Pegafishkey

Dave Alden Hutchison

Copyright © 2014 Dave Alden Hutchison

All rights reserved.

ISBN: 978-1-7373981-2-7

For the Nieces...

May your wishes be your destiny!

Monty was a happy horse, who loved to gallop swiftly through the fields and frolic in the wildflowers.

He was fast and strong and liked to listen to his friend Lindsay giggle as she rode on his back over fences and streams.

One day he looked up into the skies and saw a great eagle soaring through the clouds.

"You are so lucky to be able to fly like that," Monty told the eagle.

"Yes, I am very lucky indeed," the eagle agreed.

"It must be such fun," Monty said. "If only there were some way I could fly too."

"You could always visit the Wizard of the Willows and ask him to grant you three wishes," the eagle suggested as he stratched at the ground with his talons.

Monty had never heard of this wizard and thought for a moment that the eagle was joking.

"Not at all," said the eagle. "He is a very wise old monkey who lives many miles northwest of here. He sits under a willow tree, high upon a hill, granting wishes to anyone who can find him."

Monty told Lindsay about the wise old monkey, and she promised to help him find the willow tree on the hill.

Early the next morning, Lindsay packed a big lunch for them, took out her compass and showed Monty which direction they should go.

It was a long journey, and Monty was very tired by the time they got

to the top of the mountain, but sure enough there was an old

monkey waiting for them under a willow tree.

And he most certainly looked wise.

"Oh Wizard of the Willows, I wish I had wings so that I could fly just like a bird," Monty said.

"You mean you want to be a Pegasus?" the wise old monkey said.

Monty was confused.

"What's a Pegasus?" he asked.

"A horse with wings," the monkey said with a chuckle.

"Yes!" Monty said. "That's exactly what I want to be."

So the Wizard of the Willows held a hairy brown coconut over his head and shook it very hard until --POOF--

Monty became a Pegasus!

He was very excited as he flapped his new wings and flew through the air with Lindsay on his back.

She squealed with delight as they soared over tall mountains and small towns.

Weeks later, Monty was flying over the ocean when he spotted a school of salmon.

"I think I know what I want my second wish to be," he told Lindsay.
"I want to be able to swim and breathe underwater just like a fish."

So that night, they flew northwest toward the willow on the hill.

The flight made Monty very tired, because even though

he had wings like a bird, he was also a very heavy horse.

"I think I'll gallop the rest of the way," Monty said as they arrived at the bottom of the hill.

Once they got to the top, Monty made his request.

"You mean you want to be a Pegafish?" the wise old monkey said with a laugh.

"Yes," Monty said. "If a Pegafish is a horse that can fly and swim underwater, then that is exactly what I want to be."

So the monkey granted Monty his second wish.

Monty was very happy indeed.

He dove into the nearest lake and swam deep under the water with his new fins, breathing through his new gills.

"Yum!" he said, as he munched on the kelp that grew at the bottom of the lake.

It was very peaceful and beautiful under the water.

It was very late by the time Monty was done swimming.

Lindsay wanted to go home, but she could no longer ride on Monty's back because his fins were in the way.

"I guess I know what my third wish will be," Monty said. "I want to be a Pegafishkey."

The monkey was not laughing.

"I've never even heard of a Pegafishkey. What is that?" the confused old monkey asked.

"It's a horse that flies and swims under the sea and has hands like a monkey so he can carry a good friend around with him."

"Of course," said the monkey.

And he shook his magic coconut in the air until--POOF!

Monty flew through the air holding Lindsay securely in his new hands.

When they were halfway home, Monty felt too tired
to fly anymore, so he decided to gallop the rest of the way.

"Oh dear," he told Lindsay.
"I can't gallop and carry you at the same time."

"It's okay," Lindsay said. "I can walk the rest of the way."

"But even galloping sort of hurts my hands," Monty said. "I can't run very well. I can't fly very well. I don't do anything very well. I'm starting to think asking to be a Pegafishkey was a big mistake."

So Lindsay and Monty walked back up the mountain and asked the wise old Wizard of the Willows to turn Monty back into a horse.

The old monkey fell over with laughter.

"I can't," he said. "You used up all three of your wishes."

Monty was very sad.

"You mean I'm stuck being a Pegafishkey for the rest of my life?" he asked.

"I'm afraid so," the monkey said.

"Well, what am I supposed to do now?"

"Well," said the monkey, "If I were you…"

"Yes?" Monty said.

"I would run… I would fly… I would swim…
I guess I'd just be happy being a Pegafishkey."

Monty thought about it long and hard…

"Yes," Monty decided.

He scooped Lindsay up in his arms
and turned to go home.

"It's not such a bad thing."

About this Book

The unique look of these illustrations was created by scanning
my grandmother's quilting scraps, baskets and other
textures and layering them in Photoshop.

I hope you enjoyed reading it as much
as I enjoyed creating it for you.

It has been a true privilege!

-Dave Alden Hutchison

www.ingramcontent.com/pod-product-compliance
Lightning Source LLC
Chambersburg PA
CBHW042106090526

44590CB00004B/116